This book belongs

_____

_____

Pronunciation Guide

Barfi: Bur-fee

Chintu: Cheen-too

Choti: Chho-tee

Dhanteras: Dhun-terus

Diwali: Dee-waa-lee

Diya: Dee-yaa

Kum Kum: Koom-koom

Laddoo: Ludd-doo

Mausi: Mau-see

Mubarak: Moo-baa-ruk

Namaste: Naa-mus-te

Ravan: Raa-vun

Ram: Raam

Rangoli: Run-goalie

Note for parents: Our books provide a glimpse into the beautiful cultural diversity of India, including occasional mythology references. Given India's size and diversity, Diwali is celebrated in a multitude of different ways. In this book, we showcase elements of the 5 days of Diwali that are best suited for young readers to follow.

Diwali
50 ACTIVITY BOOK

Storytime, Dance-along, Craft, Recipes,
Puzzles, Word games, Coloring & More!

Written by:
Ajanta & Vivek

Raise Multicultural Kids

Welcome to Culture Groove!

Dear Parents, Educators & Young Readers,

Thank you for exploring Culture Groove's 5 Days of Diwali Activity Book! We've created a one-stop kit for all your Diwali teaching and celebration needs.

From storytime, dance-along and recipes to puzzles, word games, craft and coloring activities, this book has it all.

Our mission, quite simply, is to help **Raise Multicultural Kids**. Whether it's through our classes, digital resources or books, we work tirelessly to help kids everywhere see the world with a multicultural lens. This lens, in turn, helps them develop understanding, empathy, and curiosity about the world.

As parents of a young kid who is growing up outside of India, we are also very aware of the need to help better **connect kids to their roots**. We hope our work helps you as well.

Lastly, our content is not religious. It is specially focused on highlighting the cultural aspects of this beautiful festival.

Wishing you a very **Happy Diwali** from our family to yours!

Ajanta, Vivek & Ruhaan

50 Diwali Activities

1. Meet your Friends
2. Read the Diwali Book
3. It's Storytime
4. Diwali Flash Cards
5. Color the Fireworks
6. Chintu's Giftbox
7. Spot the Missing Fragment
8. Help Maya draw a silly face on Diya
9. Neel's Word search
10. Help Chintu find his Barfi
11. Diwali Sing-Along
12. Tic tac toe
13. Connect the dots
14. Make as many words
15. Pick 2 identical Chintus
16. Fill the boxes
17. Roll & Read
18. Color by number
19. Find the missing letters
20. Spot the 8 differences
21. Diya Craft
22. Learn Diwali words
23. Handprint Fireworks Craft
24. Diya Train
25. Diwali Secret Message
26. Stairs and Ladders
27. Barfi Recipe
28. Color a Rangoli
29. Diwali Riddles
30. Diwali word grid
31. Diwali Dance-Along
32. Help Ram get to Ravan
33. Veggie Rockets
34. My Diwali Journal
35. Maya's Diwali Crossword
36. Find Diwali Items
37. Diwali Playdough Fun
38. Beginning Sounds
39. Diwali spot and color
40. How many Diyas can you find?
41. Draw the other half
42. Bhai/ Behen/ Friend Dooj
43. Diwali Photo Frame
44. Find the Top View
45. Unscramble Words
46. Diwali Lantern Craft
47. Celebration Tracker
48. Shapes & Fireworks
49. Make Chintu Facemask
50. Diwali Jigsaw Puzzle

1. Meet your Friends

Meet Maya, the girl who goes on an adventure to India to celebrate Diwali!

Meet Neel, the boy who goes on an adventure to India to celebrate Diwali!

Meet Chintu, the pet squirrel, who joins Maya & Neel on all their adventures!

And together... they celebrate Diwali!

2. Read the Diwali Book
(BEST-SELLER)

Hey Kids!

You know about the **12 Days of Christmas**.
Now learn about the...
5 days of Diwali — India's Festival of Lights!

In this **multicultural** and **educational** series from Bollywood Groove, join Maya, Neel and their pet squirrel, Chintu, as they visit their Aunty Eesha in India to celebrate 5 Days of Diwali.

You will learn about Dhanteras (day 1), Choti Diwali (day 2), Diwali (day 3), Saal Mubarak (day 4) and Bhai Dooj (day 5) through this fun and beautifully illustrated story.

You will also learn about food, language and cultural elements of India... all while making two new best friends!

GET ON AMAZON WORLDWIDE:
CultureGroove.com/books

3. It's Storytime!

Join Maya, Neel and Chintu on their Diwali adventure with this Read-Aloud video!

FIND IT ON OUR CULTURE CHANNEL
CultureGroove.com/Diwali

4. Diwali Flashcards

To download and make colored Diwali flash cards,
Visit: CultureGroove.com/Diwali

Day 1

Dhanteras

Buy Pots, Pans & Jewelry

Day 2

Chhoti Diwali

Make Rangoli & Eat Sweets

Day 3

Day 4

Day 5

Diwali

Light Diya & Fireworks

Saal Mubarak

Give New Year Gifts

Bhai Dooj

Celebrate Sibling Bond

5. Color the fireworks

6. Chintu's Giftbox

Which pattern will Chintu get when
he folds his Saal Mubarak gift box?

To learn more about Saal Mubarak,
see "Day 4" in the "Let's Celebrate 5 Days of Diwali" book.

Answers at the end

7. Spot the missing fragment

Find the missing piece to decorate with flowers for Diwali

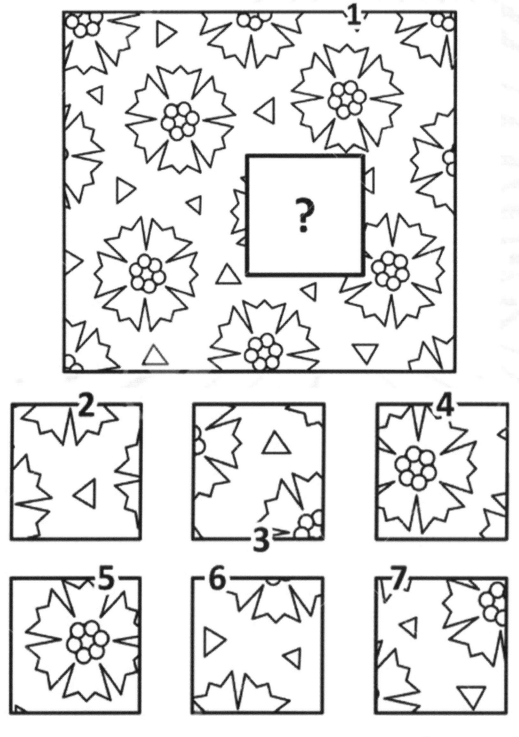

Answers at the end

8. Help Maya draw & color a silly face on the two Diyas

9. Neel's Word Search

```
O  R  T  F  Z  U  O  P  R  F  S  J
S  A  R  E  T  N  A  H  D  A  Y  O
C  K  Q  L  L  D  Y  J  A  T  I  O
H  F  R  E  A  K  A  L  O  L  V  D
I  C  E  O  S  D  M  H  O  C  E  I
N  N  S  S  W  U  D  G  Y  Q  U  A
T  D  V  W  B  E  N  O  T  W  A  H
U  F  C  A  B  A  R  W  O  A  Y  B
K  N  R  A  R  A  D  I  W  A  L  I
C  A  R  A  V  L  Y  T  F  X  B  O
K  F  I  M  X  A  L  I  E  M  W  X
I  I  V  O  S  K  F  A  D  T  K  G
```

HELP NEEL FIND THESE WORDS

Barfi	Diya	Neel
Bhai Dooj	Fireworks	Rangoli
Chintu	Laddoo	Saal Mubarak
Dhanteras	Laxmi	
Diwali	Maya	

Answers at the end

10. Help Chintu find his Barfi

11. Diwali Sing-Along

Let's sing this song, to the tunes of 12 Days of Christmas!

On the first day of Diwali, my Mausi gave to me,
A pot, pan and jewelry.

On the second day of Diwali, my Mausi gave to me,
Two yummy laddoos and a pot, pan and jewelry.

On the third day of Diwali, my Mausi gave to me,
Three clay Diyas, Two yummy laddoos and a pot, pan and jewelry.

On the fourth day of Diwali, my Mausi gave to me,
Four New Year gifts, Three clay Diyas, Two yummy laddoos and a pot, pan and jewelry.

On the fifth day of Diwali, my Mausi gave to me,
Five Bhai Dooj hugs, Four New Year gifts, Three clay Diyas, Two yummy laddoos and a pot, pan and jewelry.

FIND IT ON OUR CULTURE CHANNEL
CultureGroove.com/Diwali

12. Play Tic Tac Toe

13. Connect the dots

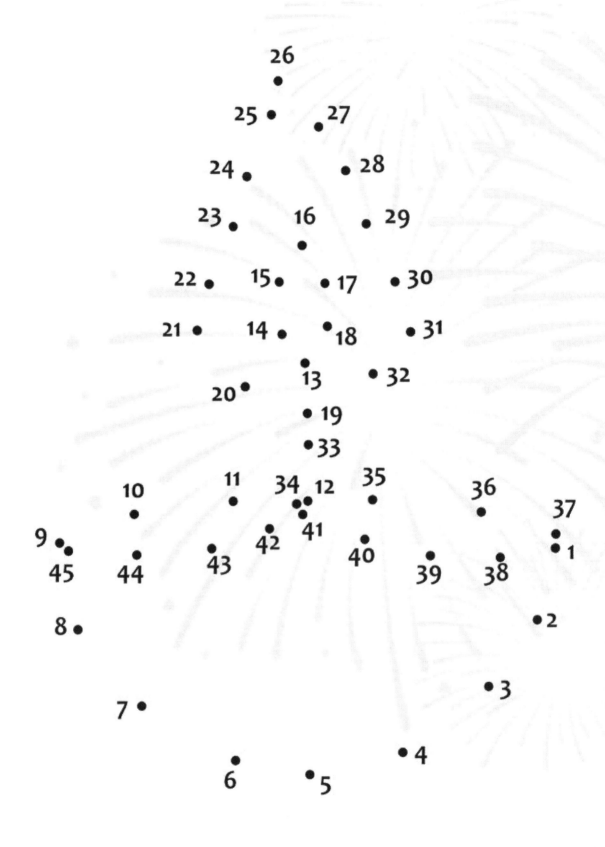

14. How many words can you make with the word "Diwali"?

| D | I | W | A | L | I |

1.	6.
2.	7.
3.	8.
4.	9.
5.	10.

Answers at the end

15. Find 2 identical Chintus

16. Fill the boxes

Fill up the boxes with the words: AID, ALMUB, DIW, CHI, FI, GOLI, LAX, NTE to reveal the Diwali words.

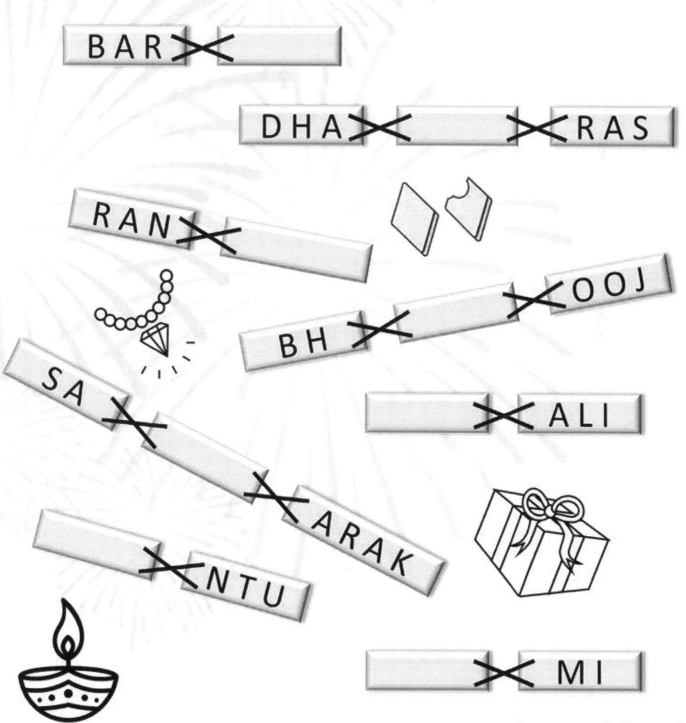

Answers at the end

17. Roll & Read

Roll a dice. Choose the activity based on the number on the dice. Color and cross it off when you complete it. If you don't have the book, be creative!

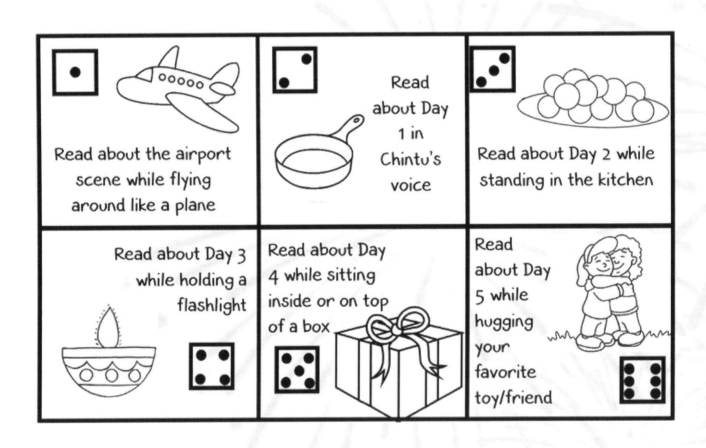

Read about the airport scene while flying around like a plane

Read about Day 1 in Chintu's voice

Read about Day 2 while standing in the kitchen

Read about Day 3 while holding a flashlight

Read about Day 4 while sitting inside or on top of a box

Read about Day 5 while hugging your favorite toy/friend

To get the book "Let's Celebrate 5 Days of Diwali!", please visit
CultureGroove.com/books
Available worldwide on Amazon in Kindle, paperback and hard cover

18. Color by number

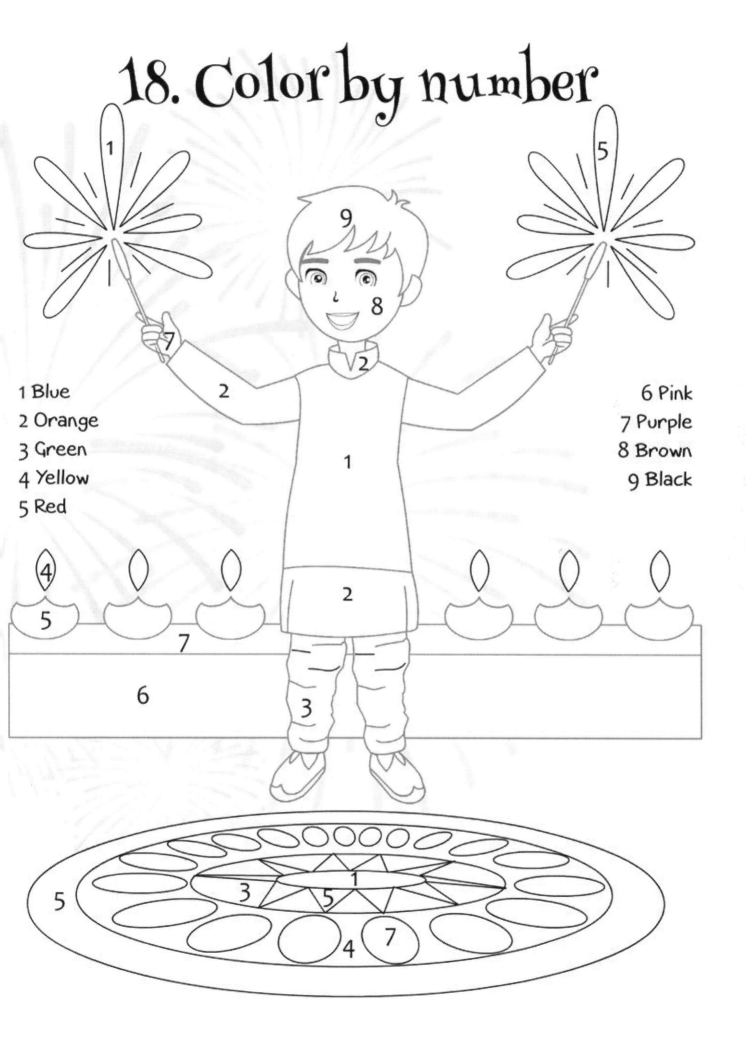

1 Blue
2 Orange
3 Green
4 Yellow
5 Red

6 Pink
7 Purple
8 Brown
9 Black

19. Find the missing letters

Diwali is the festival of __ights.

5

It is celebrated for __ive days.

It is the biggest festival of __ndia.

It celebrates victory of King Ram over __avan.

It is celebrated by lighting __ireworks.

Answers at the end

20. Spot 8 differences

Answers at the end

21. Diya Craft

Make this easy Diya (clay lamp) craft.
Add a festive touch to your space!

FIND IT ON OUR CULTURE CHANNEL
CultureGroove.com/Diwali

22. Learn Diwali Words

Diya ----------> Clay lamp

Rangoli ----------> Drawing with colored powder

Laddoo ----------> Round sweet

Laxmi ----------> Goddess of Money

Barfi ----------> Square-shaped sweet

Saal Mubarak ----------> Happy New Year

23. Handprint Fireworks

Make your own Diwali fireworks wall art.
It is also a great activity to do for baby's first Diwali!

Materials: 2 Cardstocks, Picture frame, Paint

Steps:

☐ On a cardstock, paint streaks using various colors.
This is your fireworks background.

☐ Now put color on your child's or baby's hand and make
a handprint on another cardstock.

☐ Cut out the shape of the handprint and glue it to the
fireworks background.

☐ Put it in a nice picture frame and write Happy Diwali!

24. Diya Train

Write down one word that
reminds you of each day of Diwali.

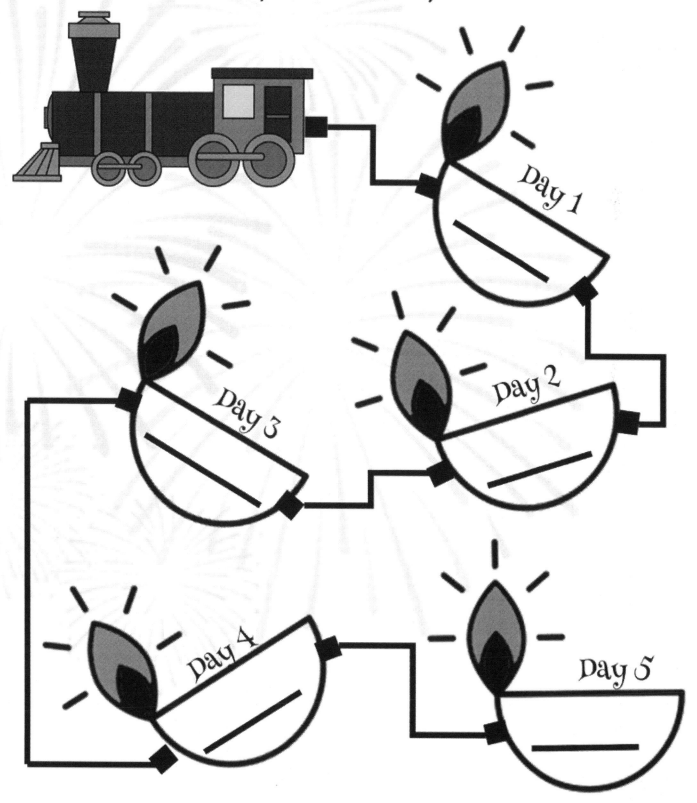

Day 1

Day 2

Day 3

Day 4

Day 5

25. Diwali Secret Message

Discover the secret Diwali message
by using the decoding key from below

⊕ ◊ Φ Φ 8   Ш ∧ ∫ ◊ ₪ ∧   □ ⊏

8 ⊏ ↓   ◊ ∞ Ш   8 ⊏ ↓ ∂   Ω ◊ ↑ ∧ ₪ 8

DECODING KEY

A	B	C	D	E	F	G	H	I	J
◊	X	o	Ш	∨	Ω	‖	⊕	∧	Σ
K	L	M	N	O	P	Q	R	S	T
⌂	₪	↑	∞	⊏	Φ	↔	∂	∩	□
U	V	W	X	Y	Z				
↓	ϙ	∫	Ϭ	8	☉				

Answers at the end

26. Stairs & Ladders

Using the stairs and ladders only,
find a way from A to B. Do not jump or climb.

27. Barfi Recipe

Ingredients

2.5 cups of grated coconut

1.25 cups of sugar

1 cup milk

1 teaspoon Ghee

1/8th teaspoon cardamom powder

How to make your Diwali barfi

☐ Put grated coconut in a bowl

☐ Add sugar and mix

☐ Warm Ghee in a pan

☐ Add coconut & sugar

☐ Stir until sugar melts

☐ Add milk and keep stirring

☐ Add cardamom powder

☐ Take the mix off the gas once it's dry enough

☐ Place wax paper on a baking dish

☐ Pour the mix on the baking dish

☐ Flatten to even out the surface

☐ Garnish with almond flakes

☐ Cut into cubes while still hot

☐ Enjoy! Yummmm....

Barfi Recipe contd.

Watch the coconut barfi recipe online

FIND IT ON OUR CULTURE CHANNEL
CultureGroove.com/Diwali

28. Color a Rangoli

Rangoli is made with colored powder.
People usually draw it near their house doors
Color your own Rangoli!

29. Diwali Riddles

Turns the nighttime into day,
This pretty thing is made of clay.

What is it?

A great new beginning, marks the New Year,
This day after Diwali, is filled with gifts and cheer.

What is it?

Near the front door, it is often seen,
Pattern drawn with powders of red, yellow and green.

What is it?

Shaped like a very precious rock,
This sweet food is the color of chalk.

What is it?

Answers at the end

30. Diwali Word Grid

Help Chintu fill the grids with these words

DIYA   GIFT
SAAL   CLAY
FIRE   BARFI
LAMP   LAXMI

D I W A L I

R A N G O L I

I
F
T

M U B A R A K

Answers at the end

31. Diwali Dance-Along

Get your dancing feet ready!
Watch and Dance-along to this fun Diwali song

FIND IT ON OUR CULTURE CHANNEL
CultureGroove.com/Diwali

32. Help Ram get to Ravan

33. Veggie Rockets

*Make veggies fun
with this veggie rocket*

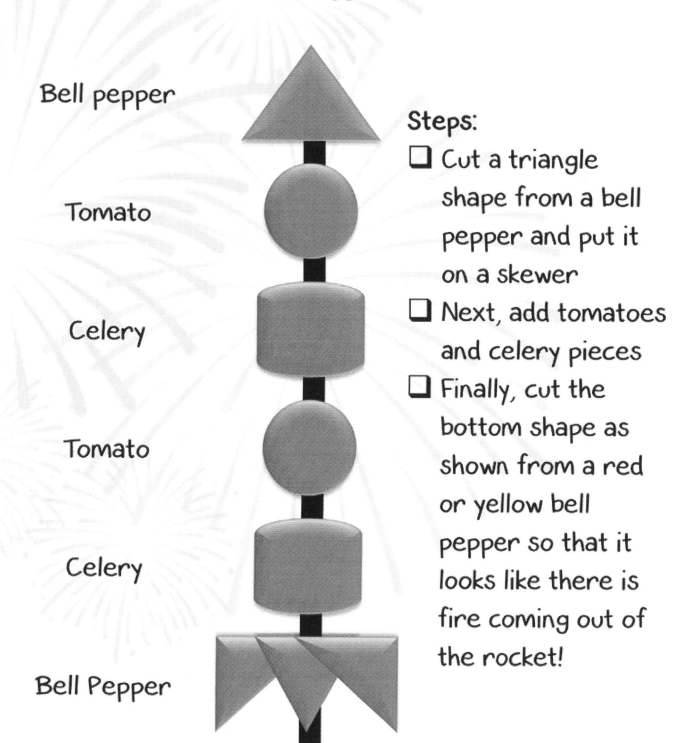

Bell pepper

Tomato

Celery

Tomato

Celery

Bell Pepper

Steps:
- [ ] Cut a triangle shape from a bell pepper and put it on a skewer
- [ ] Next, add tomatoes and celery pieces
- [ ] Finally, cut the bottom shape as shown from a red or yellow bell pepper so that it looks like there is fire coming out of the rocket!

34. My Diwali Journal

I ate...

_____

_____

_____

_____

I learned...

_____

_____

_____

_____

How did you celebrate? Feel free to decorate with stickers and drawings.

I made...

_____

_____

_____

_____

I read/watched...

_____

_____

_____

_____

35. Maya's Diwali Crossword

Across
1. Day 4 of Diwali
2. Colored Powder Drawing
3. Square or diamond-shaped Diwali sweets
4. Goddess of Money

Down
1. Diwali clay lamp
2. Day 1 of Diwali
3. Festival of Lights
4. Round Diwali sweets
5. Makes a "BOOM" sound
6. Day 5 of Diwali

Answers at the end

36. Find Diwali Items

Can you find all the items related to Diwali?
Think of all 5 days and what we do on those days.

Answers at the end

37. Diwali Playdough Fun

Make this pattern with playdough.
Place a Diya or a tealight where it's marked with "D".

38. Beginning Sounds

What word describes the item?
Color the first letter of that word.

Answers at the end

39. Diwali Spot & Color

Answer the following questions as you color the next page:

☐ What do we buy on Day 1 of Diwali? Color them after you find them!

☐ What is the round object on the plate for Day 2?

☐ Can you find the Diya in this picture?

☐ On what day of Diwali do you exchange gifts?

☐ What gift would you gift someone on Day 4?

☐ Do you see the brother and sister giving each other a hug on Day 5? What is Day 5 of Diwali called?

Answers at the end

Spot & Color contd.

40. How many Diyas can you find?

41. draw the other half

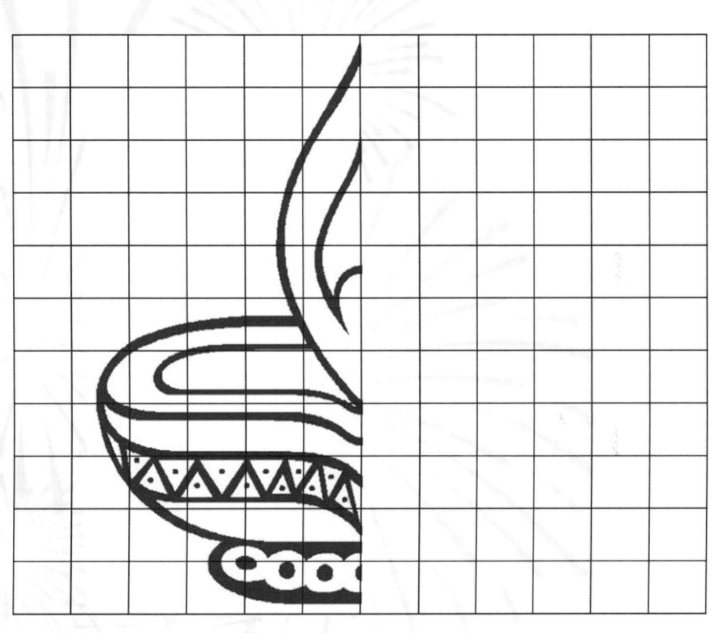

42. Bhai/Behen/Friend Dooj

*Celebrate the special sibling,
cousin or friendship bond through Bhai Dooj!*

What you need:

- ☐ A plate – ideally made out of metal
- ☐ Felt paper – two different colors
- ☐ Self-adhesive gems or any other decorative material
- ☐ Two tiny bowls
- ☐ Rice
- ☐ Kumkum or red face paint
- ☐ Diya or tealight candle

Getting your Bhai Dooj plate ready:

- ☐ Cut a circle from felt paper as big as the inside of the plate and place it on the plate.
- ☐ Cut petal shapes from another felt paper and place them to create a pattern as shown.
- ☐ Add gems or other items to further decorate the plate.
- ☐ Add rice to one tiny bowl and Kumkum or red face paint to another bowl.
- ☐ Light a Diya or a tealight candle and place it on the plate.

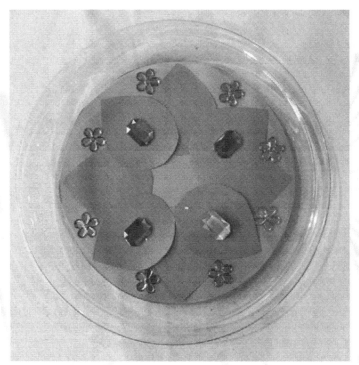

To celebrate:

- ☐ Sit down with your sibling, cousin or friend with the plate in between.
- ☐ Dip your ring finger in Kumkum or red paint and make a petal like shape on their forehead. This is called a Teeka.
- ☐ Stick a couple of rice grains on the Teeka.
- ☐ Next, have your sibling, cousin or friend do the same to you.
- ☐ Give each other a hug if you wish and promise to always be there for them!

43. Diwali Photo Frame

Materials

- ☐ Foam pieces of different colors
- ☐ Glue gun
- ☐ scissors

Steps

- ☐ Cut a big piece of flame from red foam.
- ☐ Cut a smaller piece of flame from orange foam.
- ☐ Cut the smallest piece of flame with yellow foam.
- ☐ Glue them one on top of the other as shown in the picture.
- ☐ Next cut the shape of a bigger Diya using your favorite color.
- ☐ Now cut a smaller Diya shape of any color. Cut a circle in the middle of it.
- ☐ Using glue gun, attach the three flames with the bigger Diya shape.
- ☐ Stick the two Diyas, only in the spots shown with dotted circles.
- ☐ Using glue gun, stick the picture frame to a thick piece of oval-shaped foam. The oval-shaped foam is the base.

Diwali Photo Frame contd.

☐ Cut shapes of a star from a foam of any color and stick them on your picture frame.

☐ Slide a picture from the top and your picture frame is ready!

44. Find the top view

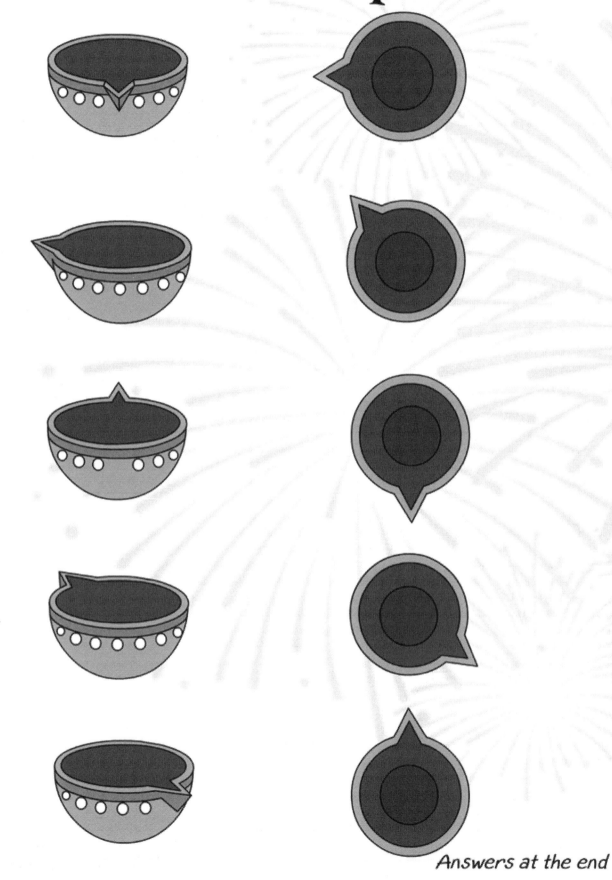

Answers at the end

45. Unscramble words

BFIAR

_____

IABH OJOD

_____

CITNUH

_____

TRANDSHEA

_____

IIAWDL

_____

IYDA

_____

REKORFSIW

_____

DOLADO

_____

AMXIL

_____

AAYM

_____

ELEN

_____

NAIRGOL

_____

LSAA UAKRAMB

_____

Answers at the end

46. Diwali Lantern

Material

- ☐ Colored paper or glitter paper
- ☐ Gems with self-adhesive back
- ☐ Scissors, stapler
- ☐ Glue stick, ruler

Steps

- ☐ Take a square sheet of paper and fold it in half.
- ☐ Draw straight lines with a ruler that are about one inch apart.
- ☐ Cut straight lines with scissors. Make sure the cut doesn't extend till the edge. Leave a gap of about an inch from the edge.

Diwali Lantern contd.

- ❏ Open the page. Roll it and staple at the end.

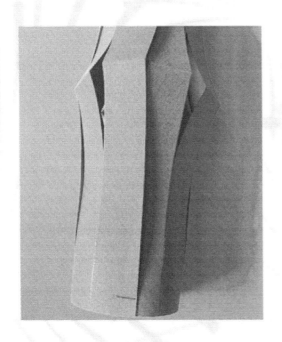 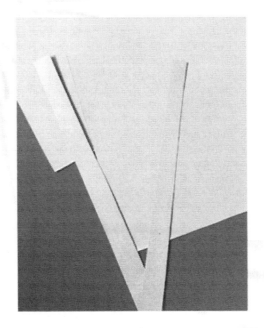

- ❏ Cut strips of a different color.
- ❏ Attach at the top & bottom.
- ❏ Decorate with gems or any other decorative items.

47. Celebration Tracker

Complete your 5 Day Checklist

	Day 1	Day 2	Day 3	Day 4	Day 5
I read					
I made					
I solved					
I learned					

48. Shapes & Fireworks

Cut & color these shapes. Then glue them
together to make your own rocket firework... WHOOSH!

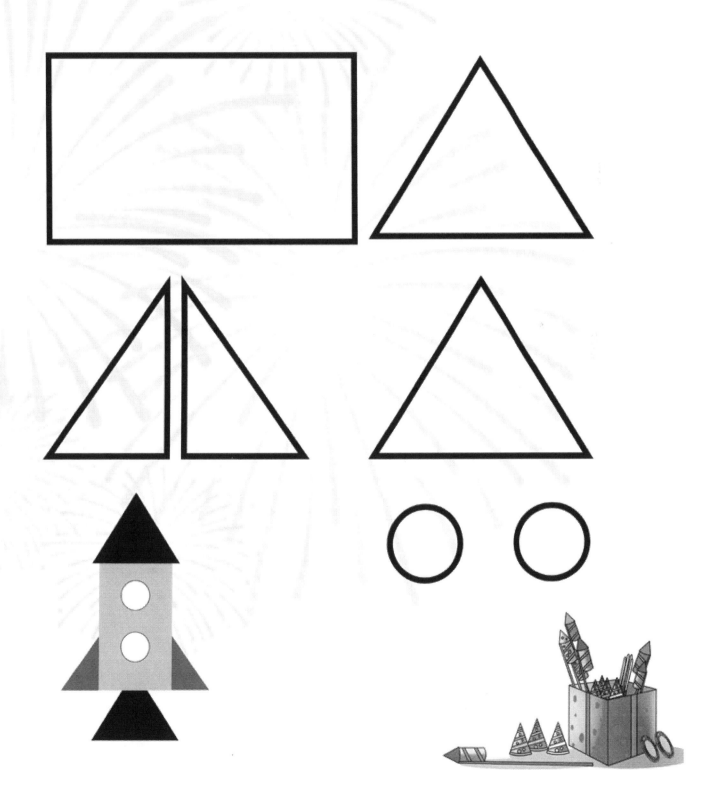

This page is intentionally left blank

49. Chintu Facemask

Cut out the shape. Cut out the eyes.
Punch two holes on the side.
Attach a string or rubber band.

This page is intentionally left blank

50. Diwali Jigsaw Puzzle

Cut the image along the dotted lines. Jumble the pieces. Have fun putting the picture together!

This page is intentionally left blank

Answer Key

6. Chintu's Giftbox

Box 3

7. Spot the missing fragment

Box 4

9. Neel's Word Search

14. Words with 'DIWALI'

AID	LAW
AIL	LID
DIAL	WAD
LAD	WAIL
LAID	WILD

14. Fill the boxes

BAR<u>FI</u>
DHA<u>NTE</u>RAS
RANG<u>OLI</u>
BHAI D<u>OO</u>J
<u>DIW</u>ALI
SA<u>AL</u> MUBARAK
<u>CH</u>INTU
LA<u>XM</u>I

19. Find the missing letters

<u>L</u>ight, <u>F</u>ive, <u>I</u>ndia, <u>R</u>avan, <u>F</u>ireworks

20. Spot the 8 differences

Answer Key cont.

25. Diwali Secret Message

Happy Diwali to you and your family

29. Diwali Riddles

- ☐ Diya
- ☐ Saal Mubarak
- ☐ Rangoli
- ☐ Barfi

30. Word Grid

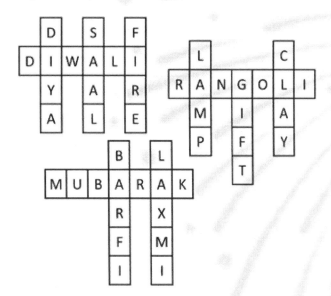

35. Maya's Crossword

ACROSS
1. SAALMUBARAK
2. RANGOLI
3. BARFI
4. LAXMI

DOWN
1. DIYA
2. DHANTERAS
3. DIWALI
4. LADDOO
5. FIREWORKS
6. BHAIDOOJ

36. Find Diwali Items

38. Beginning Sounds

R, F, G
R, C, L
D, B, P

39. Spot & Color

- ☐ Pots, pans & jewelry
- ☐ Laddoo
- ☐ N/A
- ☐ Day four
- ☐ N/A
- ☐ Bhai Dooj

Answer Key cont.

44. Find the top view

45. Unscramble Words

BARFI	LADDOO
BHAI DOOJ	LAXMI
CHINTU	MAYA
DHANTERAS	NEEL
DIWALI	RANGOLI
DIYA	SAAL
FIREWORKS	MUBARAK

Thank you & Happy Diwali!

If you enjoyed this Activity book, check out our other titles...

About the Authors

Ajanta Chakraborty was born in Bhopal, India, and moved to North America in 2001. She earned an MS in Computer Science from the University of British Columbia and also earned a Senior Diploma in Bharatanatyam, a classical Indian dance, to feed her spirit.

Ajanta quit her corporate consulting job in 2011 and took the plunge to run Bollywood Groove (and also Culture Groove) full-time. The best part of her work day includes grooving with classes of children as they leap and swing and twirl to a Bollywood beat.

Vivek Kumar was born in Mumbai, India, and moved to the US in 1998. Vivek has an MS in Electrical Engineering from The University of Texas, Austin, and an MBA from the Kellogg School of Management, Northwestern University.

Vivek has a very serious day job in management consulting. But he'd love to spend his days leaping and swinging, too.

We have been featured on:

We are independent authors who want to help raise multicultural kids! We rely on your support to sustain our work. Please help:

✓ Drop us an Amazon review at: **CultureGroove.com/books**

✓ Give our books as **gifts, party favors** (bulk order discounts)

✓ Schedule our unique **'Dancing Bookworms'** author visit

Many thanks!

Made in the USA
San Bernardino,
CA